PREPARATION FOR THE FINAL CRISIS

Study Work Book

FOREWORD

Brenda Hill's systematic and well-outlined Study Work Book closely parallels the Scriptural research of Dr. Fernando Chaij in his book <u>Preparation for the Final Crisis</u>. This Study Work Book encourages a deeply personal Bible study. It is an excellent resource for use in spiritual growth groups. Such guided in-depth Bible study develops reflection, self-examination and sharing of what the Word of God means to us. It also promotes the personal application of each person's beliefs and values, and challenges the student to live by these.

Fernando Chaij and my father, Nicolas Chaij, were very close brothers. Their special bond was formed when my father, Nicolas, shared with Fernando his new-found faith and his excitement with the Bible truths he had discovered in the Seventh-day Adventist Church. This changed their lives and their relationships forever. From then on they committed their lives to the Lord. They chose to attend the Adventist College in Argentina and both became pastors, educators and writers of the gospel message they loved.

Thus, Fernando Chaij represents more to me than an uncle. His unwavering faith in Jesus was strengthened by continuous study and research of the Scriptures. Whenever any decision or issue had to be faced, he searched the Bible to understand God's will. He loved to share spiritual insights with others, and he would be delighted with Brenda Hill's Study Work Book for the <u>Preparation for the Final Crisis</u>.

This Study Work Book faithfully captures the spirit of the <u>Preparation for the Final Crisis</u>. It stimulates the mind through step-by-step moments of meditation and clarification. Such illumination of the gospel increases our spiritual discernment and in-depth perception. It will add hours of spiritual joy in the renewed discovery of God's plan.

Selma A. Chaij-Mastrapa, Ph.D.

Study Work Book Endorsements

"No study of end-time events is complete that does not include practical application to one's own spiritual life. Brenda Hill's Study Work Book achieves this combination very effectively. I know from experience that a workbook such as this is an excellent way both to develop a relationship with Jesus and to develop a godly character -- the two elements that will be present in the lives of all those who remain faithful to God through earth's final hours."
-- **Marvin Moore**, author
The Crisis of the End Time

"The big question before us today is How shall we do Scripture? Serious study of the Word is 'where it's at.' We need every good resource we can put our hands on that will help us to get into the Word, because it is the Word that strengthens us. . . . Brenda Hill's Study Work Book is right on target, well organized, easy to negotiate. It is relevant, all about what is happening now, and what to expect tomorrow. . . . The spoon-fed Christian who neglects to set aside quality time to hear his Lord speak through the Word will be blown away in the coming storm."
-- **Charles Bradford**
Former North American Division President

"Brenda Hill's Study Work Book for <u>Preparation for the Final Crisis</u> is definitely a user-friendly study work book that will no doubt inculcate students with our present truth message. Bible and spirit of prophecy-centered, this Study Work Book is good not only for new Adventists, but will help those who have been in the message for a long time. It really takes the Bible and makes it relevant for us today."
-- **Clifford Goldstein**, author
Day of the Dragon

"Thoughtful response to the challenging appeals of this Study Work Book is guaranteed to foster faith and fortify one for present and future conflict."
-- **Calvin Rock**, General Vice President
General Conference of Seventh-day Adventists

"<u>Preparation for the Final Crisis</u> by Fernando Chaij represents the powerful and solid Seventh-day Adventistism that I was brought upon and still cherish. Brenda Hill's fine Study Work Book is well done and should prove very valuable both for study and for rich spiritual development."
-- **Mervyn Maxwell**, Professor of Church History
Andrews University Seminary

Edited by Brenda D. Hill
Cover Design by Ron Pride

Copyright © 1997 by
Pacific Press® Publishing Association
All rights reserved. No part of this
book may be reproduced in any form without
written consent of the publisher.
Printed in the United States of America

ISBN 13: 978-0-8163-1564-2
ISBN 10: 0-8163-1564-7

ABOUT THIS STUDY WORK BOOK

The purpose of this Study Work Book is to assist you, the reader, in your study of the Bible and the spirit of prophecy as it pertains to last day events as outlined in the text <u>Preparation for the Final Crisis</u>.

Originally, this Study Work Book was designed for my personal use because I am a visual learner and handwriting information seems to help me retain that information moreso than just reading it. I do think that there may be others who learn in this manner therefore I have made this Study Work Book available.

The first chapter and the sixth chapters are the longer chapters in the text, therefore those chapters in the Study Work Book are also longer.

You will note chapter one begins with many definitions and texts to be completed. However, there are five ways to respond to the questions and statements in this Study Work Book:

1. Write out Scripture.
2. Fill in the blank on spirit of prophecy quotations which are taken from the text.
3. True and False answers.
4. Researching your Bible to respond to questions.
5. Personal application (hopefully thought-provoking) questions.

May this Study Work Book serve its purpose -- to assist you in the retention of God's Holy Word, that your declaration may be:

"Thy word have I hid in mine heart,
that I might not sin against Thee."
Psalm 119:11

TABLE OF CONTENTS

Introduction . . . . *i*

Acknowledgments . . . . *ii*

Chapter 1: Reform Movement Within the Church. 1

Chapter 2: The Sealing 23

Chapter 3: The Latter Rain 33

Chapter 4: The Shaking 46

Chapter 5: The Finishing of God's Work--The Loud Cry . . . 58

Chapter 6: Persecution--The Confederated Power 67

Chapter 7: The Work of Deception--Spiritualism 102

Chapter 8: The Early Time of Trouble 118

Chapter 9: The Time of Trouble 124

Chapter 10: The Plagues 141

Chapter 11: The End of the Seventh Plague--Deliverance . . . 150

Chapter 12: From the Liberation to the Second Coming of Christ . . 156

Chapter 13: Preparation for the Crisis 172

Appendix:

End Time Books and Resources

Order Form

~ INTRODUCTION ~

*"Study to shew thyself approved unto God,
a workman that needeth not to be ashamed,
rightly dividing the word of truth."
-- II Timothy 2:15*

This Study Work Book will require intensive Bible study and study of the spirit of prophecy as you read the text <u>Preparation for the Final Crisis</u>.

The subject matter itself demands diligence, for we are preparing for the final crisis -- to stand alone. In the <u>Great Controversy</u> under the chapter entitled "The Scriptures A Safeguard," we are counseled:

> "It is the first and highest duty of every rational being to learn from the Scriptures what is truth, and then to walk in the light, and encourage others to follow his example. We should day by day study the Bible diligently, weighing every thought, and comparing Scripture with Scripture. With divine help, we are to form our opinions for ourselves, as we are to answer for ourselves before God." (page 598)

> "None but those who have fortified the mind with the truths of the Bible will stand through the last great conflict. To every soul will come the searching test, Shall I obey God rather than men?" (pages 593-594)

It is my desire that this Study Work Book will serve as a tool to assist you in your studies as you prepare to meet our Lord and Saviour, Jesus Christ.

Brenda D. Hill
Douglassville, PA
1994

~ *Acknowledgments* ~

to

My Lord and Saviour, Jesus Christ

Praise and honor to our Lord and Saviour, Jesus Christ for the privilege of presenting a tool of encouragement to those who love Him and look forward to His coming.

Praise and honor to our Lord and Saviour, Jesus Christ for a godly husband and determined God-fearing parents.

To Pastor Byron K. Hill, Sr.

My deepest gratitude, and much love, to my husband, Byron, who encouraged me from conception to fruition of this project. I thank God daily for you.

My Parents, Elder Henry and Mrs. Earline Smith

My eternal love and gratitude to my loving and wise parents, Henry and Earline Smith, who 'rooted' my feet on the path of this blessed truth while I was still cradled in their arms attending Sabbath School Cradle Roll class at the Dupont Park Seventh-day Adventist Church in Washington, D.C. You two have been my most precious gifts from God. Thank you!

Our Children

Chonrae, Barry, Tovanne, Jamar, Byron, Courtney
with whom we want to enjoy heaven throughout eternity
Make God First!

CHAPTER 1

REFORM MOVEMENT WITHIN THE CHURCH

NAME:_____

"For the grace of God that bringeth salvation hath appeared to all men, teaching us that, denying ungodliness and worldly lusts, we should live soberly, righteously, and godly, in this present world; looking for that blessed hope, and the glorious appearing of the great God and our Saviour Jesus Christ; Who gave Himself for us, that He might redeem us from all iniquity, and purify unto Himself a peculiar people, zealous of good works."

Titus 2:11-14

Chapter 1

Reform Movement Within the Church

Write out Revelation 3:20-21

___

Define confession:

___

Write out I John 1:9

___

Personal: How do I recognize the need for confession?

___

Study Work Book for "Preparation for the Final Crisis"

Personal: What puts me into an attitude for confession?

_____

_____

_____

_____

Write out Isaiah 57:15

_____

_____

_____

_____

_____

Write out I Peter 5:6-7

_____

_____

_____

_____

Define humility:

_____

_____

_____

Personal: Why is an attitude of humility necessary?

___

Personal: What must I do to be as "He is" . . . humble?

___

Write out II Peter 3:9

___

Define repentance:

Personal: As I study the meaning of repentance, how can I obtain a spirit of repentance?

_____
_____
_____
_____

Write out Hebrews 2:1

_____
_____
_____
_____

Define repentance:

_____
_____
_____

Personal: How can I develop a more serious faith?

_____
_____
_____
_____

Study Work Book for "Preparation for the Final Crisis"

Chapter 1 - Reform Movement Within the Church

Write out Matthew 6:9

___

Define prayer:

___

Personal: What can I do to make my prayer life one of fellowship with God?

___

Write out Romans 14:9

Define revival:

_____

_____

_____

Personal: What must I rid my life of to escape spiritual death?

_____

_____

_____

Personal: Since revival in my life will only take place under the ministration of the Holy Spirit what must I do to assure the indwelling of the Holy Spirit in my life?

_____

_____

_____

_____

_____

Write out II Corinthians 3:18

_____

_____

_____

_____

Chapter 1 - Reform Movement Within the Church

Define reformation:

Personal: How can Bible study and consecration to God assist me in personal reformation?

Write out Psalm 119:88

Define quickening:

Personal: What areas of my faith need quickening?

_____
_____
_____
_____
_____
_____
_____

~ True or False ~

[] T [] F We must make an earnest effort to obtain the blessing of the Holy Spirit because sinfulness has made God unwilling to bestow this blessing upon us.

[] T [] F The Lord will not admit into the mansions He is preparing for the righteous one soul who is self-sufficient.

[] T [] F The purifying work of the reformation must first begin with the ministers.

[] T [] F Reformation can bring forth the good fruit of righteousness without revival.

[] T [] F Before the final visitation of God's judgments upon the earth there will be among the people of the Lord such a revival of primitive godliness as has not been witnessed since apostolic times.

[] T [] F True reformation does not encounter serious obstacles from the devil.

[] T [] F One way to test those who call themselves "reformers" is by the Bible text Matthew 7:16 "Ye shall know them by their fruits."

Chapter 1 - Reform Movement Within the Church

The following characteristics of Satan's counterfeit reformation are listed below. Give examples of these characteristics:

Discord and Strife:

Criticism:

Fanaticism:

"New Light":

Chapter 1 - Reform Movement Within the Church

Give a brief description of the characteristics of genuine reformation (page 32) also, respond to the personal application questions:

A Spirit of Prayer:

_____

_____

_____

_____

Personal: How is practicing the presence of God synonomous with being in an attitude or spirit of prayer?

_____

_____

_____

_____

Personal: What must I do to maintain a spirit-filled prayer life?

_____

_____

_____

_____

Personal: How can I develop a method of prayerful intercession for others?

_____

_____

_____

_____

A Spirit of Sincere Conversion:

Personal: Have I experienced genuine conversion? [] yes   [] no
If so, in what ways can I tell that I have truly experienced the "new birth"?

Personal: If not, what am I going to do to obtain conversion?

A Widespread Spirit of Self-denying Missionary Work:

Personal: Where is my mission?

Personal: What am **I** willing to deny "self" to service my mission field?

A Spirit of Praise and Thanksgiving:

Personal: For what can I praise God?

Personal: What am I thankful to God for?

_____
_____
_____
_____

Personal: How can I maintain a spirit of thankfulness?

_____
_____
_____
_____

Give a description of the "lukewarm state" (page 34) and respond to the personal application questions.

_____
_____
_____
_____

Personal: How does the above description relate to me?

_____
_____
_____

Chapter 1 - Reform Movement Within the Church *Page 14*

What are the four elements that make up the "lukewarm state" (page 35)?

1. _____
   _____

2. _____
   _____

3. _____
   _____

4. _____
   _____

Write out Revelation 3:14-15

_____
_____
_____
_____
_____
_____

What was the result of hearing this message when it was first presented (page 37)?

_____
_____
_____

Study Work Book for "Preparation for the Final Crisis"

Chapter 1 - Reform Movement Within the Church

What is the remedy of heaven for the triple affliction of Laodicea and what is the meaning of each of the remedies (pages 38-39)?

Affliction	Remedy	Meaning of Remedy

Chapter 1 - *Reform Movement Within the Church*   Page 16

Complete the following from page 38:

"The gold mentioned by Christ, the _____ _____, which all must have, has been shown me to be _____ and _____ combined, and _____ takes the precedence of _____. -- Testimonies to the Church, vol. 2, pg. 36.

Justification by Faith

Write out Hebrews 11:6

_____
_____
_____

What two ways can an individual seek righteousness?

1. _____
   _____

2. _____
   _____

Personal: How have I sought righteousness?

_____
_____
_____
_____

Study Work Book for "Preparation for the Final Crisis"

Chapter 1 - Reform Movement Within the Church

What can appear as evidences of our faith?

_____

_____

_____

_____

Personal: What are some evidences of <u>my</u> faith?

_____

_____

_____

_____

Define impute:

_____

_____

_____

Define impart:

_____

_____

_____

What is Justification by Faith?

_____

_____

_____

_____

_____

What are the two classes of righteousness?

1. _____

   _____

2. _____

   _____

List the five points given in the text of the righteousness of Christ by which we are justified (page 42).

1. _____

2. _____

3. _____

4. _____

5. _____

Chapter 1 - Reform Movement Within the Church

List the four points given of the righteousness of Christ by which we are sanctified (page 42).

1. _____

2. _____

3. _____

4. _____

~ Justification? or Sanctification ~

1. _____ - Continuing victory over sin.
2. _____ - The pardon of God.
3. _____ - Our right to heaven.
4. _____ - A linear process that progresses throughout a lifetime.

Study Work Book for "Preparation for the Final Crisis"

Chapter 1 - Reform Movement Within the Church

Complete the following statement quoted from page 47:

"Christ has given us no _____ that to attain _____ of _____ is an easy matter. A _____, all-round _____ is not _____. It does not come to us by _____. A noble _____ is _____ by _____ effort through the _____ and grace of _____. . . . It is formed by hard, stern _____ with self. Conflict after _____ must be waged against hereditary _____. We shall have to criticize _____ closely, and allow not one unfavorable _____ to remain _____." -- Christ Object Lessons, pg. 331.

How can we become impregnable to the assaults of Satan (page 48)?

_____
_____
_____
_____
_____

Write out James 4:7-8

_____
_____
_____
_____

Chapter 1 - Reform Movement Within the Church

Record several promises that will strengthen you as you go forward in the reformation and revival of this church:

Text:_____

_____
_____
_____
_____
_____

Text:_____

_____
_____
_____
_____
_____

Text:_____

_____
_____
_____
_____
_____

~ NOTES ~

CHAPTER 2

THE SEALING

"And this is love, that we walk after His commandments. This is the commandment, that, as ye have heard from the beginning, ye should walk in it. For many deceivers are entered into the world, who confess not that Jesus Christ is come in the flesh. This is a deceiver and an antichrist. Look for yourselves, that we lose not those things which we have wrought, but that we receive a full reward. Whosoever transgresseth, and abideth not in the doctrine of Christ, hath not God. He that abideth in the doctrine of Christ, he hath both the Father and the Son."

II John 6-9

Chapter 2

The Sealing

Write out II Timothy 2:19

_____

_____

_____

_____

Personal: This text says this to me about the "seal" of God:

_____

_____

_____

_____

When does *The Sealing* begin?

_____

_____

_____

When does *The Sealing* end?

_____

_____

_____

Study Work Book for "Preparation for the Final Crisis"

Chapter 2 - The Sealing

List the four objectives accomplished by *The Sealing* (page 49).

1. _____

2. _____

3. _____

4. _____

Write out Luke 16:13

_____

Define allegiance:

_____

Personal: To whom have I given my allegiance?

_____

Chapter 2 - The Sealing

Complete the following statement quoted from page 50:

"While one class, by _____ the sign of _____ to earthly _____, receive the mark of the _____, the other, choosing the token of _____ to _____ authority, receive the _____ of God." -- Great Controversy, page 605.

~ True or False ~

[] T [] F   The "latter rain" and "the refreshing from the presence of the Lord" is synonymous.

[] T [] F   In vision the prophet Ezekiel was shown the sealing of the servants of God.

[] T [] F   The mighty angel bearing the seal of God ascends from the west.

[] T [] F   The "mark of deliverance" will be set upon the men who keep God's commandments, who revere His law, and who refuse the mark of the beast or his image.

[] T [] F   God will protect every soul that has decided on the truth and are pure in heart.

What is the Seal of God?

Instrument	Mark
_____	_____
_____	_____
_____	_____
_____	_____
_____	_____
_____	_____
_____	_____

Study Work Book for "Preparation for the Final Crisis"

Who receives the Seal of God?

What is the distinction of the 4th Commandment from the other nine commandments?

Personal: What does the 4th Commandment mean to me?

Chapter 2 - The Sealing

Write out Exodus 31:12-13

_____

_____

_____

_____

_____

_____

_____

What elements of nature are being held in check by the four angels?

_____

_____

_____

Who will receive the Seal of God?

____	the humble	____	world-lovers
____	the pure	____	the honest
____	the deceitful	____	the unjust
____	liars	____	the righteous

Personal: What is Jesus doing for me in His holy temple?

_____

_____

_____

_____

Study Work Book for "Preparation for the Final Crisis"

What will be the condition of everyone after Jesus leaves His holy temple?

Write out Ephesians 6:12-17

Chapter 2 - The Sealing

Complete the following statement quoted on page 54:

"Those that overcome the _____, the _____, and the _____, will be the _____ ones who shall receive the _____ of the living God. Those whose _____ are not clean, whose _____ are not pure, will not have the seal of the living _____. Those who are _____ sin and _____ it will be passed by. Only those who, in their _____ before God, are filling the _____ of those who are _____ and _____ their sins in the great antitypical day of _____, will be recognized and marked as _____ of God's protection." -- Testimonies to Ministers, page 445.

<u>Personal:</u>   What <u>must</u> I do to overcome the world?

_____
_____
_____
_____

Write out Revelation 3:11

_____
_____
_____
_____
_____
_____

~ NOTES ~

CHAPTER 3

THE LATTER RAIN

"Hereby know we that we dwell in Him, and He in us, because He hath given us of His Spirit."

I John 4:13

Chapter 3

The Latter Rain

Write out John 14:15-16

_____
_____
_____
_____

[]T []F   Without the Holy Spirit not a single soul will be converted.

List some of the functions of the Holy Spirit:

1. _____

2. _____

3. _____

4. _____

5. _____

6. _____

Study Work Book for "Preparation for the Final Crisis"

Chapter 3 - The Latter Rain

Write out Psalm 51:10-11

___

Personal: How have I allowed the Holy Spirit to work in my life?

___

Personal: How can I secure a repentant heart?

___

Personal: How can I allow the Holy Spirit to direct me in my Bible studies?

___

Study Work Book for "Preparation for the Final Crisis"

Chapter 3 - The Latter Rain

Personal: When tempted how can I use as my defense "it is written" instead of using my own form of defense?

Personal: How can I maintain a consistent prayer life?

Personal: What proof do I have that I am a child of God?

Personal: How has **my** witnessing been effective?

Study Work Book for "Preparation for the Final Crisis"

Chapter 3 - The Latter Rain

Write out Luke 11:13

_____
_____
_____
_____

What is the purpose of the "early rain"?

_____
_____
_____
_____

Which refer to the "early rain"?

_____ seedtime   _____ spiritual grace

_____ refreshing from   _____ harvest time
      the Lord

_____ Day of Pentecost   _____ Holy Spirit

Although different in time and purpose, how is the "early rain" comparative to the "latter rain"?

_____
_____
_____
_____
_____

Study Work Book for "Preparation for the Final Crisis"

Chapter 3 - The Latter Rain

Personal: What does it mean to me to "watch and pray"?

_____
_____
_____
_____

Complete the following quoted from page 58:

"The descent of the Holy Spirit upon the _____ is looked forward to as in the _____; but it is the privilege of the church to have it _____. _____ for it, _____ for it, _____ for it. We must have it, and _____ is waiting to bestow it." -- Evangelism, page 701

The promise of the Holy Spirit is given on condition. What are the conditions as listed in the text?

1. _____

2. _____

3. _____

4. _____

5. _____

Study Work Book for "Preparation for the Final Crisis"

Personal: When is the last time I prayed for the Holy Spirit in my life and what were the results?

_____

_____

_____

_____

_____

Personal: How can I be a laborer together with Christ?

_____

_____

_____

Personal: What should my prayer be for myself and others who attend worship services?

_____

_____

_____

_____

Personal: How do I know I've experienced the "early rain"?

_____

_____

_____

_____

Study Work Book for "Preparation for the Final Crisis"

Chapter 3 - The Latter Rain

How did the disciples prepare for the outpouring of the Holy Spirit on the Day of Pentecost?

_____
_____
_____
_____

Personal: Am I living up to all the "light" I have received?

_____
_____

Personal: How can I "daily advance in the exemplification of active Christian virtues"?

_____
_____
_____

Personal: When can I have "my vessel" purified to be ready to receive the "latter rain"?

_____

Write out Isaiah 61:11

_____
_____
_____
_____

Personal: How have I allowed the Holy Spirit to use me?

_____
_____
_____
_____

Write out Philippians 2:13

_____
_____
_____

[ ]T [ ]F Only to those who wait humbly upon God, who watch for His guidance and grace, is the Spirit given.

Personal: How can I promote unity among my brethren?

_____
_____
_____
_____

What will be the result in the life of the "one who is fully emptied of self"?

_____
_____
_____
_____

Chapter 3 - The Latter Rain

When and how often are we to renounce self?

_____
_____
_____
_____

What are two characteristics mentioned that are highly offensive to God?

1. _____
   _____

2. _____
   _____

Why are these two characteristics so offensive to God?

_____
_____
_____
_____

Complete the following quoted on page 62:

"There is no _____ to the _____ of the one, who putting _____ aside, makes room for the _____ of the _____ _____ upon his _____ and lives a life _____ _____ to God." -- Christian Service, page 254

Chapter 3 - The Latter Rain

List five results of the "latter rain"?

1. _____

2. _____

3. _____

4. _____

5. _____

Personal: Which of these results are being displayed in my life?

_____

Study Work Book for "Preparation for the Final Crisis"

Write out Acts 3:19-20

NOTES

CHAPTER 4

THE SHAKING

"For the wrath of God is revealed from heaven against all ungodliness and unrighteousness of men, who hold the truth in unrighteousness;... And even as they did not like to retain God in their knowledge, God gave them over to a reprobate mind, to do those things which are not convenient."

Romans 1:18, 28

Chapter 4

The Shaking

Write out I Peter 4:17-18

_____
_____
_____
_____
_____
_____
_____

Personal: I feel judgment must begin at the house of God because:

_____
_____
_____
_____

Define apostasy:

_____
_____
_____
_____

Chapter 4 - The Shaking

Personal: How can I avoid apostasizing?

_____
_____
_____
_____
_____
_____

Write out I Peter 5:8

_____
_____
_____

What are listed as the four basic causes of the "falling away"?

1. _____
   _____

2. _____
   _____

3. _____
   _____

4. _____
   _____

How does a child of God become careless and indifferent?

Personal: How can I avoid becoming careless and indifferent?

Write out II Timothy 3:12

What will happen to those who have not been sanctified through obedience when persecution comes upon the church of God? (page 67)

Chapter 4 - The Shaking

Personal: Of what am I fearful?

_____
_____
_____
_____

Write out Isaiah 35:3-4

_____
_____
_____
_____
_____
_____

Complete the following quoted from page 67:

"The members of the church will _____ be _____ and _____. They will be placed in circumstances where they will be _____ to bear witness for the _____. Many will be called to _____ before _____ and in courts of _____, perhaps separately and _____. The experience which would have _____ them in this _____ they have _____ to obtain, and their _____ are burdened with _____ for _____ opportunities and _____ privileges." -- Testimonies to the Church, vol. 5

Chapter 4 - The Shaking

What is the counsel of the True Witness to the Laodiceans? (Revelation 3:14-18)

_____

_____

_____

_____

Personal: How can I follow the counsel of the True Witness?

_____

_____

_____

How are "surface readers" of God's Word described?

_____

_____

_____

Personal: How can I avoid being a "surface reader"?

_____

_____

_____

What is pantheism and is it a current belief?

_____

_____

_____

Study Work Book for "Preparation for the Final Crisis"

Chapter 4 - The Shaking

Write out two Scriptures that will disprove pantheism?

Text:_____

_____
_____
_____
_____

Text:_____

_____
_____
_____
_____

What will happen to the church of God when the law is made void?

_____
_____
_____
_____

What will happen to those "branches" not connected to the True Vine?

_____
_____
_____
_____

Study Work Book for "Preparation for the Final Crisis"

Chapter 4 - The Shaking

Personal: How can I be a "living" branch?

_____
_____
_____

Write out John 15:4-5

_____
_____
_____
_____
_____

~ True or False ~

[]T []F   We are now in the shaking time.

[]T []F   Character is now being developed.

[]T []F   God is testing and proving His people.

[]T []F   Motives, during these testing times, are irrelevant.

Write out I Corinthians 10:12

_____
_____
_____

Study Work Book for "Preparation for the Final Crisis"

Chapter 4 - The Shaking   *Page 55*

List three ways to avoid "falling."

1. _____

   _____

   _____

2. _____

   _____

   _____

3. _____

   _____

   _____

~ True or False ~

[ ]T [ ]F   We must in word and deed obey the commands of God.

[ ]T [ ]F   We will be held responsible for the work we might have done but did not do because of spiritual indolence.

[ ]T [ ]F   Those who belong to the Lord's kingdom must work earnestly for the saving of souls.

<u>Personal:</u>   In what ways can I work "now" for the saving of souls?

_____

_____

_____

_____

Study Work Book for "Preparation for the Final Crisis"

Characteristics of the Overcomers	Characteristics of the Lost

Write out the following texts that give a blessed assurance of God's ability to see us through the crisis to the end.

Psalm 34:17: _____

_____

_____

Micah 7:8-9: _____

_____

_____

_____

_____

_____

I Corinthians 10:13:

Romans 8:38-39:

II Peter 2:9:

NOTES

CHAPTER 5

THE FINISHING OF GOD'S WORK
THE LOUD CRY

*"Finally, my brethren,
be strong in the Lord,
and in the power of His might.
Put on the whole armor of God,
that ye may be able to stand
against the wiles of the devil.
For we wrestle not against flesh
and blood, but against principalities, against powers,
against the rulers of the darkness of this world,
against spiritual wickedness
in high places.
Wherefore take unto you
the whole armor of God,
that ye may be able to withstand
in the evil day,
and having done all,
to stand."*

Ephesians 6:10-13

Chapter 5

The Finishing of God's Work -- The Loud Cry

Write out Matthew 24:14

What is the "Third Angel's Message"?

Describe the "Loud Cry"?

In what way will the message of the "Loud Cry" stir up persecution and controversy?

Study Work Book for "Preparation for the Final Crisis"

Chapter 5 - The Loud Cry

Personal: How can I prepare to be a participant in the "Loud Cry"?

_____

_____

_____

_____

_____

_____

Complete the following quoted from page 77:

"Thus the _____ of the _____ angel will be _____. As the time comes for it to be given with greatest _____, the _____ will work through humble _____, leading the _____ of those who _____ themselves to His _____. The laborers will be _____ rather by the unction of His _____ than by the _____ of literary _____. Men of _____ and _____ will be constrained to go forth with _____ zeal, declaring the _____ which _____ gives them. The sins of _____ will be laid open. The _____ results of _____ the _____ of the church by _____ authority, the inroads of _____, the stealthy but _____ progress of the _____ power--all will be _____. By these solemn _____ the people will be _____. Thousands upon thousands will _____ who have never _____ words like these." -- Great Controversy, page 606

Study Work Book for "Preparation for the Final Crisis"

Personal: What will it take, on my part, for the Holy Spirit to qualify me as an instrument of God?

_____

_____

_____

_____

Write out II Timothy 3:12

_____

_____

_____

What methods will be used to try and persuade God's people to turn from God?

_____

_____

_____

_____

Personal: What method of persuasion do I feel would threaten my hold on God?

_____

_____

_____

_____

Chapter 5 - The Loud Cry

What will be the result when the restraining Spirit of God shall be withdrawn from men?

What will be the benefit, during the times of persecution, of God's people having a habit of looking to God and to His Word -- alone?

Write out II Timothy 2:15

As the message is proclaimed with faith and power, what will be the response of those outside the will of God?

Chapter 5 - The Loud Cry

What will be the response of the people of God to those opposers of God's Word?

_____

_____

_____

Write out Daniel 3:16-18

_____

_____

_____

_____

_____

_____

_____

List seven people of faith, from the Word of God, who faced death because of their loyalty to God and victoriously stood their ground.

1. _____   2. _____

3. _____   4. _____

5. _____   6. _____

7. _____

Along with faith, what else did these seven people have in common?

_____

Study Work Book for "Preparation for the Final Crisis"

Chapter 5 - The Loud Cry   Page 65

Complete the following from page 79, quoted from "Testimonies to the Church," vol. 6, page 401:

"When the _____ of _____ really breaks upon us, the _____ sheep will hear the true _____ voice. _____ efforts will be put forth to _____ the lost, and many who have _____ from the fold will come back to _____ the great _____. The people of God will draw _____ and present to the _____ a _____ front. In view of the common _____, strife for _____ will cease."

Personal: In what way is it possible for me to put forth self-denying efforts to save the lost -- <u>now</u>?

_____
_____
_____
_____
_____
_____

What does John 17:21 mean to me?

_____
_____
_____
_____

Study Work Book for "Preparation for the Final Crisis"

~ NOTES ~

CHAPTER 6

PERSECUTION--

THE CONFEDERATED POWER

"And we know that all things work together for good to them that love God, to them who are the called according to His purpose."

Romans 8:28

Chapter 6

Persecution -- The Confederated Power

Write out Psalm 34:19

___

Give three definitions of "persecution."

1. ___

2. ___

3. ___

___

Write out II Timothy 3:12

___

Study Work Book for "Preparation for the Final Crisis"

Chapter 6 - Persecution

Personal: How do I interpret "godly living"?

_____
_____
_____
_____

Write out Matthew 5:10-12

_____
_____
_____
_____
_____
_____
_____
_____

~ True or False ~

[]T []F   No man can serve God without enlisting against himself the opposition of the hosts of darkness.

[]T []F   All, except the Jews, will be required to render obedience to human edicts in violation of the divine law.

[]T []F   The forms of religion will be continued by a people from whom the Spirit of God has been finally withdrawn, but it will bear the semblance of zeal for God.

Study Work Book for "Preparation for the Final Crisis"

Chapter 6 - Persecution

List three ways the enemies of God "will seek to overthrow the faith" of the children of God.

1. _____

2. _____

3. _____

Complete the following quoted from page 87:

"_____ will excite the indignation against the humble _____ who conscientiously _____ to accept popular _____ and traditions." -- Testimonies, vol. 5, page 450

Personal: What popular customs and traditions of a "spiritual" nature am I following now?

_____

Study Work Book for "Preparation for the Final Crisis"

Chapter 6 - Persecution

Complete the following quoted on page 88:

"As the _____ approaches, a large _____ who have professed _____ in the _____ angel's _____, but have not been _____ through _____ to the _____, abandon their _____ and _____ the ranks of the _____. By _____ with the world and _____ of its spirit, they have come to view matters in nearly the same _____; and when the _____ is brought, they are prepared to choose the _____, _____ side. Men of _____ and pleasing address, who once _____ in the _____, employ their powers to _____ and _____ souls. They become the most _____ _____ of their _____ brethren. When _____ keepers are brought before the _____ to answer for their _____, these _____ are the most _____ agents of _____ to _____ and accuse them, and by _____ reports and _____ to stir up the _____ against them." -- The Great Controversy, page 608

Personal: What does it mean to be "sanctified through obedience"?

_____
_____
_____
_____
_____
_____
_____

Chapter 6 - Persecution

How will ministers -- not of God -- respond to their parishioners who question them concerning the truths of God's Word they will hear?

_____
_____
_____
_____

How will the parishioners, who have been led by the ungodly ministers, respond to the answers given them by those ministers?

_____
_____
_____
_____

Write out Romans 1:20-22

_____
_____
_____
_____
_____

Complete the following quoted on page 89:

"This small _____, unable to _____ themselves in the deadly _____ with the powers of _____ that are _____ by the _____ host, make _____ their _____." -- Testimonies to the Church, vol. 5, page 213

Study Work Book for "Preparation for the Final Crisis"

Write out Psalm 7:10

_____
_____
_____

Write out Psalm 62:6-7

_____
_____
_____
_____

"Those who have step by step yielded to worldly demands and conformed to worldly customs will not find it a hard matter to yield to the powers that be, rather than subject themselves to derision, insult, threatened imprisonment, and death." -- Testimonies, vol. 5, page 81.

Personal: What worldly demands have I conformed to?

_____
_____
_____
_____

Write out Romans 12:2

_____
_____
_____

Chapter 6 - Persecution

Personal: How can I be in this world but not of this world?

_____

_____

_____

_____

What are . . .

The Commandments of God	The Commandments of Men

~ True of False ~

[]T The members of the church
[]F will individually be
tested and proved.

[]T Many will be called to
[]F speak before councils and
courts of justice,
perhaps separately and
alone.

Study Work Book for "Preparation for the Final Crisis"

Chapter 6 - Persecution

Write out Matthews 10:19-20

_____
_____
_____
_____

Write out II Timothy 2:15

_____
_____
_____

Write out John 14:26

_____
_____
_____
_____

Personal: Knowing that I may be called before councils and in courts of justice to answer for my faith what must I do to prepare for that time?

_____
_____
_____
_____

Study Work Book for "Preparation for the Final Crisis"

Chapter 6 - Persecution

Personal: What does <u>total dependence</u> on God mean to me?

_____
_____
_____
_____

Write out Revelation 3:10

_____
_____
_____
_____

Complete the following taken from pages 90-91:

"God would not suffer the _____ to destroy those who are expecting _____ and who would not _____ to the _____ of the beast or receive his _____. I saw that if the _____ were permitted to _____ the saints, _____ and all his evil _____, and all who hate _____, would be _____. And oh, what a _____ it would be for his _____ majesty to have _____, in the last _____ struggle, over those who had so long _____ to behold _____ whom they _____! Those who have _____ at the idea of the _____ going up will _____ the care of _____ for His _____ and behold their glorious _____." -- Early Writings, page 284

Study Work Book for "Preparation for the Final Crisis"

Chapter 6 - Persecution

What will be the great central theme of the controversy in the last days?

___

Write out Exodus 20:8-11

___

Personal: What do I feel are the controversial points about the fourth commandment? (Name at least two points.)

1. ___

2. ___

Study Work Book for "Preparation for the Final Crisis"

Chapter 6 - Persecution

Personal: How will these controversial points affect the relationships I have <u>now</u> with those whom I have chosen as my friends and companions?

_____

_____

_____

_____

~ True or False ~

[ ]T [ ]F   Those who keep the commandments of God and the faith of Jesus will feel the ire of the dragon and his hosts.

[ ]T [ ]F   The persistent refusal of a small minority to yield to the popular demand, of the observance of Sunday as a sacred day, will make them objects of nation-wide execration.

[ ]T [ ]F   Those who honor the Bible Sabbath will be denounced as enemies of law and order, as breaking down the moral restraints of society, causing anarchy and corruption, and calling down the judgments of God upon the earth.

[ ]T [ ]F   Ministers who deny the obligation of the divine law will present from the pulpit the duty of yielding obedience to the civil authorities as ordained of God.

[ ]T [ ]F   Only those dignitaries of the state will seek to bribe, persuade, or compel all classes to honor the Sunday.

Write out Revelation 3:11

_____

_____

_____

_____

Chapter 6 - Persecution

Personal: How can I "hold fast" so that no man will take my crown?

_____
_____
_____
_____
_____

"The class that have provoked the displeasure of Heaven will charge all their troubles upon those whose obedience to God's commandments is a perpetual reproof to transgressors." -- Great Controversy, page 590

Name three persons in Scripture who were falsely accused but lived a life of obedience to God's commandments. Also, name the trial they faced as a result of their faithfulness.

1. _____
_____
_____
_____

2. _____
_____
_____
_____

3. _____
_____
_____
_____

Study Work Book for "Preparation for the Final Crisis"

What was the outcome of the faithfulness of the three persons in Scripture you described?

1. _____

2. _____

3. _____

What are some things that will be offered to God's people as inducements to renounce their faith?

1. _____

2. _____

3. _____

4. _____

Personal: Which of these inducements are now a threat to my relationship with my Saviour?

_____
_____
_____
_____

Chapter 6 - Persecution

Write out Romans 8:38-39:

_____
_____
_____
_____

How is a "nominal Adventist" described?

_____
_____
_____

As the Sabbath is proclaimed more fully what will be the response of those who are "God's chosen" but who are not now of the Seventh-day Adventist Church (page 91)?

_____
_____
_____
_____

Complete the following from page 93:

"Church and _____ are now making preparations for the future _____. Protestants are working in _____ to bring _____ to the front, as did the Romanists. Throughout the land the _____ is piling up her lofty and massive _____, in the _____ recesses of which her former _____ are to be repeated. And the way is preparing for the _____, on a _____ scale, of those lying _____ by which, if it were possible, _____ would deceive even the _____." -- Testimonies, vol. 5, pages 449-450.

Chapter 6 - Persecution

Write out Colossians 3:12-13

_____
_____
_____
_____
_____
_____

Define transcript:

_____
_____
_____

What is the transcript of God's character?

_____

Personal: How do I view this as the transcript of the character of God?

_____
_____
_____
_____
_____
_____

Chapter 6 - Persecution

What is the fearful warning from God declaring the penalty of bowing to the beast and his image?

_____
_____
_____
_____

Personal: What does liberty of conscience mean to me?

_____
_____
_____
_____

Write out Daniel 7:25

_____
_____
_____
_____
_____

What is the "sign of authority" claimed by papal Rome?

_____
_____
_____
_____

Study Work Book for "Preparation for the Final Crisis"

Chapter 6 - Persecution

In her writings (page 94), Ellen White noted various plans the devil has conjured up to try and lead the children of God away from Him. List four of them:

1. _____

2. _____

3. _____

4. _____

~ True or False ~

[]T []F   The United States has been the great bulwark of religious liberty.

[]T []F   The United States is represented as the second beast of Revelation 13 (with horns like a lamb).

[]T []F   Every country in the world, except Israel, will follow the lead of the United States in imposing Sunday laws.

[]T []F   The substitution of the laws of men for the law of God will be the last act in the drama.

[]T []F   Although the United States leads out, the same crisis will come upon God's people in all parts of the world.

Write out Matthew 5:17-18

_____
_____
_____
_____
_____
_____
_____

Personal: When Jesus said He came to "fulfill" the law I believe He meant this:

_____
_____
_____
_____
_____

Personal: Matthew 5:18 says this to me:

_____
_____
_____
_____
_____

Chapter 6 - Persecution

What do the "lamblike" features of the United States represent:

Politically:

_____
_____
_____
_____
_____
_____
_____

Spiritually:

_____
_____
_____
_____
_____
_____
_____

How will the United States disconnect herself fully from righteousness?

_____
_____
_____
_____
_____

Chapter 6 - Persecution

How is national apostasy defined?

_____

_____

_____

_____

_____

_____

What will follow national apostasy?

_____

_____

_____

_____

_____

_____

Complete the following quoted on pages 97-98:

"While men are _____, Satan is _____ arranging matters so that the _____ people may not have _____ or _____. The _____ movement is _____ making its way in _____. The _____ are concealing the _____ issue, and many who _____ in the movement do not themselves see whither the _____ is tending. Its _____ are mild and apparently _____, but when it shall speak it will reveal the _____ of the _____." -- Testimonies to the Church, vol. 5, page 452

Chapter 6 - Persecution

Write out I Peter 4:12-13

_____

_____

_____

_____

_____

_____

Personal: How am I now handling what I consider "fiery trials" in my life?

_____

_____

_____

Write out Matthew 24:13

_____

_____

_____

Personal: What does this promise mean to me?

_____

_____

_____

_____

Study Work Book for "Preparation for the Final Crisis"

Chapter 6 - Persecution

Who/what is represented by the following as the alliance of power that is being developed against God's people?

1. The dragon _____

2. The beast _____

3. The false prophet _____

4. The state _____

Write out Revelation 12:17

_____
_____
_____
_____
_____

From page 99, how is it that Protestantism shall fill their measure of iniquity that will bring about God doing His "strange work"?

_____
_____
_____
_____
_____
_____
_____

Study Work Book for "Preparation for the Final Crisis"

Chapter 6 - Persecution

Concerning the two great errors used by the devil, provide three Bible texts that reveal the truth.

Error	Bible Text	Bible Text	Bible Text
Immortality of the Soul			
Sunday Sacredness			

~ True or False ~

[]T []F   The Scriptures teach that popery is to regain its lost supremacy.

[]T []F   The Protestant governments will not be converted to the world.

[]T []F   In order for the United States to form an image of the beast, the religious power must so control the civil government that the authority of the state will also be employed by the church to accomplish her own ends.

[]T []F   The Protestant world pays homage to the Roman Church in their acceptance of the false sabbath.

[]T []F   It is the boast of Rome that she never changes.

Personal: This is how I view the difference between Sunday exaltation and Sabbath worship:

_____

_____

_____

_____

Personal: The statement quoted on page 102 "... the greater the light bestowed, the greater the darkness of those who pervert and reject it" says to me:

_____

_____

_____

_____

Chapter 6 - Persecution

Write out Matthew 6:22

_____
_____
_____

Define gulf:

_____
_____
_____

What is the "gulf" Protestantism is reaching across as stated in the quotation on page 102: "Protestantism is now reaching hands across the gulf to clasp hands with the papacy..."

_____
_____
_____
_____
_____

How is "a mark of allegiance to the pope in place of God" described?

_____
_____
_____
_____

Chapter 6 - Persecution

Complete the following statement quoted on page 103:

"When the leading _____ of the United States, _____ upon such points of _____ as are held by them in _____, shall _____ the state to _____ their decrees and to _____ their _____, then _____ America will have _____ an _____ of the _____ hierarchy, and the _____ of civil _____ upon _____ will inevitably result." -- Great Controversy, page 445.

List three points of doctrine now common in the Protestantism.

1. _____
_____

2. _____
_____

3. _____
_____

Write out Matthew 6:24

_____
_____
_____
_____

Study Work Book for "Preparation for the Final Crisis"

Chapter 6 - Persecution

There are those who observe Sunday, sincerely believing it to be the true day of worship. God is fair and just. What does Acts 17:30 reveal?

Personal: How does this text speak to me of God's fairness?

Write out James 4:17

Personal: What does this text mean to me in light of the truths that are revealed to me through God's Word?

Personal: Are there any truths that have been revealed to me that I am not living up to? If so, why not?

_____
_____
_____

Exodus 31:13 states that the Sabbath is a sign between God and His children throughout their generations. Write out three additional texts from the New Testament that support this text.

Text: _____

_____
_____
_____
_____

Text: _____

_____
_____
_____
_____

Text: _____

_____
_____
_____
_____

~ True or False ~

[] T [] F   The light we have received upon the third angel's message is the true light.

[] T [] F   The Sabbath will be the great test of loyalty, for it is the point of truth especially controverted.

[] T [] F   The keeping of the true Sabbath, in obedience to God's law, is an evidence of loyalty to the Creator.

[] T [] F   The Sabbath is the sign of God's authority.

[] T [] F   Sunday does bear the credentials of God because God created all days.

[] T [] F   To secure popularity and patronage, legislators will yield to the demand for a Sunday law.

[] T [] F   There are now true Christians in every church who honestly believe that Sunday is the Sabbath of divine appointment.

[] T [] F   It is not until the issue is thus plainly set before the people, and they are brought to choose between the commandments of God and the commandments of men, that those who continue in transgression will receive 'the mark of the beast.'"

[] T [] F   With the issue thus clearly brought before him, whoever shall trample upon God's law to obey a human enactment receives the mark of the beast; he accepts the sign of allegiance to the power which he chooses to obey instead of God.

[] T [] F   I will not trample upon God's law.

Chapter 6 - Persecution

Complete the following from page 107:

"The _____ given me by the Lord at a time when we were _____ just such a _____ as you seem to be approaching, was that when the _____ were moved by a power from _____ to enforce _____ observance, Seventh-day Adventists were to show their _____ by refraining from their _____ work on that day, _____ it to _____ effort." -- Testimonies to the Church, vol. 9, page 232

Personal: How is the above statement <u>not</u> a compromise of my faith?

_____
_____
_____
_____
_____
_____
_____

Into what two classes will Christianity be divided?

1. _____
   _____

2. _____
   _____

Study Work Book for "Preparation for the Final Crisis"

Chapter 6 - Persecution

Write out John 15:4-5

_____
_____
_____
_____
_____
_____

Personal: We are counseled "Not one who is abiding in Christ will fail or fall." What do I need to do to continue abiding in Christ?

_____
_____
_____
_____

How long will the four angels hold the four winds?

_____
_____

What will be the result when the protection of human laws are withdrawn from those who honor the law of God?

_____
_____
_____
_____

Study Work Book for "Preparation for the Final Crisis"

Chapter 6 - Persecution

We are counseled in Selected Messages, book 2, page 141 (page 112 of the text) the following:

"Again and again the Lord has instructed that our people are to take their families away from the cities, into the country, where they can raise their own provisions; for in the future the problem of buying and selling will be a very serious one."

Personal: How can I prepare now to be ready to leave the cities when the Lord opens a way for me to leave?

Write out Matthew 6:19-21

Chapter 6 - Persecution

Personal: What treasures am I storing up in this world? How can I rid myself of these treasures?

Write out Romans 8:38-39

NOTES

CHAPTER 7

THE WORK OF DECEPTION:

SPIRITUALISM

"But I would not have you to be ignorant, brethren,
concerning them which are asleep,
that ye sorrow not, even as others which have no hope.
For if we believe that Jesus died and rose again,
even so them also which sleep in Jesus
will God bring with Him.
For this we say unto you by the word of the Lord,
that we which are alive and remain unto the coming of
the Lord shall not prevent them which are asleep.
For the Lord Himself shall descend from heaven
with a shout, with the voice of the archangel,
and with the trump of God:
and the dead in Christ shall rise first:
then we which are alive and remain
shall be caught up together with them in the clouds,
to meet the Lord in the air:
and so shall we ever be with the Lord.
Wherefore comfort one another with these words."

I Thessalonians 4:13-18

Chapter 7

The Work of Deception: Spiritualism

Write out Matthew 24:24

Define spiritualism

Write out Psalm 119:11

Personal: In what ways can I "hide" God's Word in my heart?

Study Work Book for "Preparation for the Final Crisis"

Chapter 7 - The Work of Deception -- Spiritualism

Why is it necessary to be firmly rooted in the truth **via** the study of the Word of God?

_____
_____
_____
_____
_____

What will lead men to believe that the mighty works of Jesus, when He was on earth, were accomplished by magic?

_____
_____
_____
_____

Complete the following quoted on page 115:

"As _____ more closely _____ the nominal _____ of the day, it has greater power to _____ and _____. Satan himself is converted, after the _____ order of things. He will appear in the _____ of an _____ of light. Through the agency of _____, miracles will be wrought, the _____ will be healed, and many undeniable _____ will be performed. And as the _____ will profess _____ in the _____, and manifest _____ for the institutions of the _____, their work will be accepted as a _____ of _____ power." -- Great Controversy, page 588.

Chapter 7 - The Work of Deception -- Spiritualism

> Define miracle
>
> _____
>
> _____
>
> _____

Personal: How can I be assured that a miracle is of God?

_____

_____

_____

_____

Write out I Timothy 4:1-3

_____

_____

_____

_____

_____

Personal: What does I Timothy 4:1-3 say to me?

_____

_____

_____

_____

Study Work Book for "Preparation for the Final Crisis"

~ True or False ~

[ ] T [ ] F   While appearing to the children of men as a great physician, who can heal all their maladies, Satan will bring disease and disaster, until populous cities are reduced to ruin and desolation.

[ ] T [ ] F   Satan, in working his lying wonders, will bring down fire from heaven.

[ ] T [ ] F   There is no danger in tampering with spiritualism simply out of curiosity.

[ ] T [ ] F   The line of distinction between professed Christians and the ungodly is now hardly distinguishable.

[ ] T [ ] F   Miracles are a certain sign of the true church.

[ ] T [ ] F   So closely will the delusions of the antichrist resemble the true that it will be impossible to distinguish between them except by the Holy Scriptures.

[ ] T [ ] F   Those who have broken their covenant with God will, in the day of great delusions, be without God and without hope.

Write out II Thessalonians 2:9-12

_____
_____
_____
_____
_____
_____
_____
_____
_____
_____
_____

Personal: What does it mean to me to have "pleasure in unrighteousness"?

_____
_____
_____
_____

What is the danger in believing in spiritual manifestations?

_____
_____
_____
_____

What communications from the spirits will be presented?

_____
_____
_____
_____

Because "love" will be dwelt upon as the chief attribute of God, what three attributes of God will be overlooked?

1. _____

2. _____

3. _____

Chapter 7 - The Work of Deception -- Spiritualism

Complete the following quoted on page 118:

"We have reached the _____ of the last days, when some, and yes many, shall _____ from the _____, giving heed to seducing _____ and doctrines of devils. Be _____ in regard to what you _____ and how you _____. Take not a particle of interest in _____ theories. Satan is waiting to steal a _____ upon everyone who _____ himself to be _____ by his _____. He begins to _____ his power over them just as soon as they _____ to _____ his theories." -- Medical Ministry, pages 101-102

Write out Luke 21:34-36:

_____
_____
_____
_____
_____
_____
_____

Personal: What does Luke 21:36 say to me?

_____
_____
_____
_____

Study Work Book for "Preparation for the Final Crisis"

Chapter 7 - The Work of Deception -- Spiritualism

Where and how was the foundation of spiritualism laid?

_____
_____
_____
_____

What form of spiritualism has this foundation led to?

_____
_____
_____
_____

How has the acceptance, by those involved in spiritualism, of the Bible and Jesus made spiritualism more dangerous?

_____
_____
_____

What does the following quote (page 119) suggests concerning the deceitful artistry of Satan: "The prince of darkness, . . . adapts his temptations to men of all classes and conditions."

_____
_____
_____
_____

Study Work Book for "Preparation for the Final Crisis"

Chapter 7 - The Work of Deception -- Spiritualism

There is a statement on pages 119-120, of the text, that reads: "He *(meaning the devil)* appeals to the reason by the presentation of elevating themes; he delights the fancy with enrapturing scenes; and he enlists the affections by his eloquent portrayals of love and charity. He excites the imagination to lofty flights, leading men to take so great pride in their own wisdom that in their hearts they despise the Eternal One."

Personal: What forms of entertainment or recreation appeal to me **now**?

Personal: What appeals to me when I attend worship services? And could Jesus enjoy the type of services I enjoy?

Write out James 3:15 which tells why those led by Satan to take pride in their own wisdom will despise God in their hearts.

Chapter 7 - The Work of Deception -- Spiritualism

Complete the following from page 120:

"Fearful sights of a _____ character will soon be _____ in the heavens, in token of the _____ of _____ demons. The spirits of _____ will go forth to the kings of the _____ and to the whole _____, to fasten them in _____, and urge them on to _____ with Satan in his last _____ against the _____ of heaven. By these agencies, _____ and _____ will be alike _____. Persons will arise pretending to be _____ Himself, and _____ the title and _____ which _____ to the world's _____. They will perform wonderful _____ of healing and will profess to have _____ from _____ contradicting the _____ of the _____." -- Great Controversy, page 624.

Write out II Corinthians 11:14-15

_____
_____
_____
_____
_____
_____
_____
_____

Chapter 7 - The Work of Deception -- Spiritualism

Describe the "crowning act" in the great deception.

_____
_____
_____
_____

Describe the Second Coming of Jesus.

_____
_____
_____
_____

Support your description of the Second Coming with at least four Bible texts.

Text:_____

_____
_____
_____
_____

Text:_____

_____
_____
_____
_____

Text: _____

_____

_____

_____

_____

Text: _____

_____

_____

_____

_____

Write out Psalm 25:9-10

_____

_____

_____

_____

Personal: Why is a meek person teachable?

_____

_____

_____

_____

Personal: What do I need to do in my life, now, to develop a meek and teachable spirit?

Personal: What is the "fatal security" people are being lulled into and how can I avoid this trap?

Personal: What evidence do I have that the truth of righteousness has been confirmed in my life?

Write out Matthew 24:22, 25

Write out Mark 13:22

_____

_____

_____

Write out John 6:37

_____

_____

_____

Write out II Timothy 2:19

_____

_____

_____

"Only those who have been diligent students of the Scriptures and who have received the love of the truth will be shielded from the powerful delusion that takes the world captive." -- Great Controversy, page 625. (Quoted on page 122 of the text.)

Personal: What do I need to adjust in my life to become a diligent student of the Scriptures?

_____

_____

_____

_____

Write out Psalm 119:11

_____
_____
_____
_____

Notes

_____
_____
_____
_____
_____
_____
_____
_____
_____
_____
_____
_____
_____
_____
_____
_____
_____

Study Work Book for "Preparation for the Final Crisis"

CHAPTER 8

THE EARLY TIME OF TROUBLE

"They that trust in the Lord shall be as mount Zion, which cannot be removed, but abideth forever."

Psalm 125:1

Chapter 8

The Early Time of Trouble

Write out Psalm 27:1-5

_____

_____

_____

_____

_____

_____

_____

_____

_____

_____

_____

_____

Personal: My favorite of these verses is:

_____

_____

_____

_____

_____

Chapter 8 - The Early Time of Trouble

Personal: What does it mean to me to have the Lord as the Strength of my life?

When does the Early Time of Trouble begin?

When will the Early Time of Trouble end?

Write out the characteristics of this period and give a Bible prophecy which predicts that characteristic.

Characteristics of the Early Time of Trouble	Bible Prophecy

Chapter 8 - The Early Time of Trouble

Complete the following from page 124:

"At that time, while the work of _____ is closing, _____ will be coming on the _____, and the _____ will be _____, yet held in check so as not to _____ the work of the third _____." -- Early Writings, pages 85-86

Write out Luke 21:36

_____
_____
_____
_____
_____

<u>Personal:</u> What does it mean to me to "watch" as Jesus instructed in Luke 21:36?

_____
_____
_____

NOTES

_____
_____
_____
_____

Study Work Book for "Preparation for the Final Crisis"

CHAPTER 9

THE TIME OF TROUBLE

"Many

are the afflictions

of the

righteous:

but the

Lord

delivereth him

out of them all."

Psalm 34:19

Chapter 9

The Time of Trouble

Write out Isaiah 41:10

___

Define probation:

___

When will probation close for the world?

___

Chapter 9 - The Time of Trouble

Personal: What should I be doing during this probationary period?

_____

_____

_____

_____

_____

_____

_____

_____

Complete the following quoted on pages 128-129:

"An angel returning from the _____ earth announces that his work is done; the _____ test has been brought upon the _____, and all who have _____ themselves _____ to the _____ precepts have received 'the _____ of the living _____.' Then _____ ceases His _____ in the _____ above. He lifts His _____ and with a _____ voice says, 'It is done'; and all the _____ host lay off their _____ as He makes the _____ announcement: 'He that is _____, let him be unjust _____: and he which is _____, let him be filthy _____: and he that is _____, let him be righteous _____: and he that is _____, let him be holy _____.' Revelation 22:11. Every case has been _____ for _____ or _____." -- Great Controversy, page 613.

Study Work Book for "Preparation for the Final Crisis"

Personal: What does Revelation 22:11 say to **me**?

Give the parallel between the activities of the Jewish nation, when God's presence was withdrawn, and the activities of the world when the Spirit of God is finally withdrawn.

Define impenitent:

Personal: In what area(s) of my life am I impenitent?

_____
_____
_____

What is the remedy for impenitence?

_____
_____
_____
_____

Give four Bible texts to support your remedy for impenitence.

Text:_____

_____
_____
_____
_____

Text:_____

_____
_____
_____
_____

Chapter 9 - The Time of Trouble

Text:_____

_____
_____
_____
_____

Text:_____

_____
_____
_____
_____

What are the four angels holding back?

_____
_____
_____
_____

When will the angels "let go"?

_____
_____
_____
_____

Chapter 9 - The Time of Trouble *Page 131*

Although it may not appear to be, why has there been a restraint on the activities of Satan and his followers?

_____

_____

_____

_____

_____

Complete the following statement quoted on page 131:

"When He leaves the _____, darkness covers the inhabitants of the _____. In that _____ time the _____ must live in the _____ of a holy God without an _____. The _____ which has been upon the _____ is removed, and Satan has entire _____ of the finally _____. God's _____ has ended. The world has _____ His mercy, _____ His love, and _____ upon His law. The wicked have passed the _____ of their _____; the Spirit of God, persistently _____, has been at last _____. Unsheltered by _____ grace, they have not _____ from the wicked one. Satan will then _____ the inhabitants of the _____ into one _____, final _____. As the _____ of God _____ to hold in check the _____ winds of human _____, all the elements of _____ will be let loose. The whole _____ will be involved in _____ more terrible than that which came upon _____ of old." -- Great Controversy, page 614.

Chapter 9 - The Time of Trouble

What is an intercessor?

_____

_____

_____

Personal: What does it mean to me that the righteous will be without an Intercessor?

_____

_____

_____

_____

Although the righteous will be without an Intercessor, give two Scriptural promises that guarantee that the righteous will continue to have the protection of God?

Text:_____

_____

_____

_____

_____

Text:_____

_____

_____

_____

_____

Study Work Book for "Preparation for the Final Crisis"

Chapter 9 - The Time of Trouble *Page 133*

Concerning this quote on page 132 of the text answer the personal application question that follows (chart form): "The 'time of trouble, such as never was,' is soon to open upon us; and we shall need an experience which we do not now possess and which many are too indolent to obtain." -- Great Controversy, page 622.

Personal: What experiences do I need to obtain in my personal life as I seek to prepare, spiritually, for this terrible time of trouble?

In Evangelism	In My Personal Walk with God

Study Work Book for "Preparation for the Final Crisis"

~ True or False ~

[] T [] F Sunday legislation, the threefold alliance, and the repudiation of the principles of the American Constitution will be signs to us that the limit of God's forbearance is reached.

[] T [] F When Jesus' work is done in the sanctuary, the four angels will let go the four winds.

[] T [] F Jacob's experience during that night or wrestling and anguish represents the trial through which the people of God must pass just before Christ's second coming.

[] T [] F The Protestant world today see in the little company keeping the Sabbath a Mordecai in the gate.

[] T [] F Only the poor and ignorant will be cast into the most unjust and cruel bondage.

[] T [] F The saints of God will suffer great mental anguish.

[] T [] F As Satan accuses the people of God on account of their sins, the Lord permits him to try them to the uttermost.

[] T [] F Had not Jacob previously repented of his sin in obtaining his birthright by fraud, God would not have heard his prayer and mercifully preserved his life.

[] T [] F God will overlook unfaithfulness in the minor affairs of our lives.

[] T [] F All who endeavor to excuse or conceal their sins, and permit them to remain upon the books of heaven, unconfessed and unforgiven, will be overcome by Satan.

Chapter 9 - The Time of Trouble

Write out Hebrews 11:6

_____
_____
_____
_____

Personal: How can my faith be increased?

_____
_____
_____
_____

Why will this time of trouble be permitted?

_____
_____
_____
_____

Complete the following statement quoted on page 137:

"Many will be _____ away to _____ before the _____ ordeal of the time of _____ shall come upon our _____. This is another reason why we should say after our earnest _____: 'Nevertheless not my _____, but Thine, be done.' Luke 22:42." -- Counsels on Health, page 375.

Chapter 9 - The Time of Trouble

Write out Isaiah 57:1

Personal: I see God's mercy in the above statements as follows:

Personal: Knowing that God loves me and will do what is best for my salvation, how should I end my petitions to Him?

Write out Matthew 16:26

Study Work Book for "Preparation for the Final Crisis"

Chapter 9 - The Time of Trouble

Complete the following statement quoted on page 138:

"I was shown that it is the _____ of God that the _____ should cut loose from every _____ before the time of trouble comes, and make a _____ with God through _____. If they have their property on the _____ and earnestly _____ of God for _____, He will _____ them when to _____ of these things. Then they will be _____ in the time of trouble and have no _____ to weigh them down." -- Early Writings, pages 56-57.

Personal: What is an "encumbrance" in my life <u>now</u> and what covenant do I need to make (and keep) with God, <u>now</u>?

_____
_____
_____
_____
_____
_____

Write out Isaiah 33:15-16

_____
_____
_____
_____
_____
_____
_____

Personal: What does Isaiah 33:15-16 say to me?

_____

_____

_____

_____

_____

List the wonderful methods used by God to preserve His people in the past.

TEXT	Person/People	Method of Preservation
Genesis 6-8		
Daniel 3		
Daniel 6		
I Kings 17		
Acts 12		
Acts 14:19-20		

Chapter 9 - The Time of Trouble

Write out Psalm 71:3

_____

_____

_____

_____

Complete the following statement quoted on page 141:

"I saw a _____ that God was _____ over His _____ to _____ them in the time of trouble; and every _____ that was _____ on the _____ and was _____ in heart was to be _____ with the _____ of the _____." -- Early Writings, page 43.

Personal: What do I have to fear of this time of trouble?

_____

_____

_____

Write out II Corinthians 4:17-18

_____

_____

_____

_____

_____

_____

~ NOTES ~

CHAPTER 10

THE PLAGUES

"Watch ye therefore,

and pray always,

that ye may be

accounted worthy

to escape

all these things

that shall come to pass,

and to stand before the

Son of man."

Luke 21:36

Chapter 10

The Plagues
(Focusing on the 6th & 7th Plagues)

Write out Psalm 91:1-2

_____
_____
_____
_____
_____

Define plague:

_____
_____
_____
_____

Write out Psalm 91:9-10

_____
_____
_____
_____
_____

Chapter 10 - The Plagues

Read Revelation 16 and describe the results of the seven angels pouring out "the vials of the wrath of God upon the earth."

1. _____

2. _____

3. _____

4. _____

5. _____

6. _____

7. _____

Study Work Book for Preparation for the Final Crisis

Chapter 10 - The Plagues

What is the difference between the 2nd plague and the 3rd plague?

_____
_____
_____
_____

What is the response of those who are afflicted with the 4th plague?

_____
_____
_____
_____

Compare

Revelation 16:10	Revelation 13:2
"And the fifth angel poured out his vial upon the seat of the beast; and his kingdom was full of darkness; and they gnawed their tongues for pain."	"And the beast which I saw was like unto a leopard, and his feet were as the feet of a bear, and his mouth as the mouth of a lion: and the dragon gave him his power, and his seat, and great authority.

What does the "seat of the beast" represent?

_____
_____
_____
_____

Study Work Book for Preparation for the Final Crisis

Personal: Revelation 16:15 reads: "Behold, I come as a thief. Blessed is he that watcheth, and keepeth his garments, lest he walk naked, and they see his shame." This warning/promise says to me:

_____

_____

_____

_____

_____

Why are the judgments of God, prior to the close of probation, considered to be mingled with mercy?

_____

_____

_____

_____

Write out Amos 8:11-12

_____

_____

_____

_____

_____

_____

_____

Chapter 10 - The Plagues

Complete the following statement quoted from page 145:

"Others rushed to the _____ of God and _____ to be _____ how they might escape His _____. But the saints had _____ for them. The last _____ for sinners had been _____, the _____ agonizing _____ offered, the last _____ borne, the last _____ given." -- Early Writings, page 281.

Personal: After reading pages 145-146 of the text, this is my conclusion about Armageddon:

_____
_____
_____
_____
_____
_____
_____

What will be the result of the earth being lightened with the glory of the angel of Revelation 18?

_____
_____
_____
_____

Write out Matthew 16:26

___

Personal: It is stated on page 149 of the text that the wicked "have sold their souls for earthly riches and enjoyments, and have not sought to become rich toward God." How can I become rich toward God?

___

How will the wicked respond to the "false shepherds" they have allowed to lead them to destruction?

___

Write out Lamentations 3:21-23

___

~ NOTES ~

CHAPTER 11

THE END OF THE SEVENTH PLAGUE: DELIVERANCE

"Wait on the Lord,

and keep His way,

and he shall exalt thee

to inherit the land:

when the wicked are cut off,

thou shalt see it."

Psalm 37:34

Chapter 11

The End of the Seventh Plague: Deliverance

Write out Nahum 1:7

_____

_____

_____

Complete the following statement quoted on page 152:

"The _____ of God--some in _____ cells, some hidden in solitary _____ in the _____ and the _____--still plead for divine _____, while in every quarter companies of _____ men, urged on by hosts of _____ angels, are preparing for the work of _____. It is now, in the _____ of utmost extremity, that the God of _____ will interpose for the _____ of His _____." -- Great Controversy, page 635.

Personal: The following is a testimony of a time of utmost extremity wherein God delivered me.

_____

_____

_____

_____

_____

Write out Isaiah 40:9-10

Personal: The quote on page 153 of the text (Testimonies to the Church, page 354) states: "The captivity of the righteous is turned, . . ." The most recent demonstration of this in my life is as follows:

~ True or False ~

[] T [] F   The sun, moon, and stars will be shaken by the voice of God.

[] T [] F   Glorious will be the deliverance of those who have patiently waited for His coming and whose names are written in the book of life.

[] T [] F   Angry multitudes will gaze upon the symbol of God's covenant and long to be shielded from its overpowering brightness.

[] T [] F   Like Stephen the righteous will look up steadfastly into heaven and see the glory of God and the Son of man seated upon His throne.

[] T [] F   Once the wicked realize the error of their way, they will confess and be granted salvation.

[] T [] F   All who have died in the faith of the third angel's message come forth from the tomb glorified, to hear God's covenant of peace with those who have kept His law.

[] T [] F   Demons will acknowledge the deity of Christ and tremble before His power, while men are supplicating for mercy and groveling in abject terror.

[] T [] F   The voice of God will be heard from heaven, declaring the day and hour of Jesus' coming, and delivering the everlasting covenant to His people.

[] T [] F   The wicked will not be able to look upon the righteous.

[] T [] F   A blessing will be pronounced on those who have honored God by keeping His Sabbath holy.

Chapter 11 - The End of the 7th Plague: Deliverance

Complete the following quoted on page 157:

"Soon there appears in the _____ a small black _____, about half the size of a man's _____. It is the _____ which surrounds the _____ and which seems in the distance to be _____ in darkness. The people of _____ know this to be the _____ of the _____ of man. In solemn _____ they gaze upon it as it draws nearer the _____, becoming lighter and more _____, until it is a great white _____, its base of _____ like consuming _____, and above it the _____ of the covenant. Jesus _____ forth as a mighty _____. . . . As the _____ cloud comes still nearer, every _____ beholds the _____ of life." -- Great Controversy, page 640

Write out II Peter 3:9

_____
_____
_____
_____

~ NOTES ~

_____
_____
_____

Study Work Book for "Preparation for the Final Crisis"

CHAPTER 12

FROM THE LIBERATION TO THE SECOND COMING OF CHRIST

"Therefore be ye also ready:

for in such an hour

as ye think not

the Son of man

cometh."

Matthew 24:44

Chapter 12

From the Liberation to the Second Coming of Christ

Write out Revelation 22:14

_____
_____
_____
_____
_____
_____
_____

Personal: This promise assures me that:

_____
_____
_____
_____

Chapter 12 of the text *Preparation for the Final Crisis* is a recapitulation of the events of the final days of earth's history as outlined in *The Great Controversy*, pages 635-661 and *Early Writings*, pages 285-291.

The following pages are taken from *The Great Controversy*, pages 635-647, and should be used as references in answering the **True and False** questions that will make up the latter portion of this chapter.

"When the protection of human laws shall be withdrawn from those who honor the law of God, there will be, in different lands, a simultaneous movement for their destruction. As the time appointed in the decree draws near, the people will conspire to root out the hated sect. It will be determined to strike in one night a decisive blow, which shall utterly silence the voice of dissent and reproof. . . .

"With shouts of triumph, jeering, and imprecation, throngs of evil men are about to rush upon their prey, when lo, a dense blackness, deeper than the darkness of the night, falls upon the earth. Then a rainbow, shining with the glory from the throne of God, spans the heavens, and seems to encircle each praying company. The angry multitudes are suddenly arrested. Their mocking cries die away. The objects of their murderous rage are forgotten. With fearful forebodings they gaze upon the symbol of God's covenant, and long to be shielded from its overpowering brightness.

"It is at midnight that God manifests His power for the deliverance of His people. The sun appears, shining in its strength. Signs and wonders follow in quick succession. The wicked look with terror and amazement upon the scene, while the righteous behold with solemn joy the tokens of their deliverance. Everything in nature seems turned out of its course. The streams cease to flow. Dark, heavy clouds come up, and clash against each other. In the midst of the angry heavens is one clear space of indescribable glory, whence comes the voice of God like the sound of many waters, saying, 'It is done.'

"That voice shakes the heavens and the earth. There is a mighty earthquake, 'such as was not since men were upon the earth, so mighty an earthquake and so great.' The firmament appears to open and shut. The glory from the throne of God seems flashing through. The mountains shake like a reed in the wind, and ragged rocks are scattered on every side. There is a roar as of a coming tempest. The sea is lashed into fury. There is heard the shriek of the hurricane, like the voice of demons upon a mission of destruction. The whole earth heaves and swells like the waves of the sea. Its surface is breaking up. Its very foundations seem to be giving way. Mountain chains are sinking. Inhabited islands disappear. The seaports that have become like Sodom for wickedness, are swallowed up by the angry waters. Babylon the Great hath come in remembrance before God, 'to give unto her the cup of the wine of the fierceness of His wrath.' Great hailstones, every one 'about the weight of a talent,' are doing their work of destruction. The proudest cities of the earth are laid low. The lordly palaces, upon which the world's great men have lavished their wealth in order to glorify themselves, are crumbling to ruin before their eyes. Prison walls are rent asunder, and God's people, who have been held in bondage for their faith, are set free.

"Graves are opened, and 'many of them that sleep in the dust of the earth' 'awake, some to everlasting life, and some to shame and everlasting contempt.' All who have died in the faith of the third angel's message come forth from the tomb glorified, to hear God's covenant of peace with those who have kept His law. 'They also which pierced Him,' those that mocked and derided Christ's dying agonies, and the most violent opposers of His truth and His people, are raised to behold Him in His glory, and to see the

Chapter 12 - Liberation to Second Coming of Christ

honor placed upon the loyal and obedient.

"Thick clouds still cover the sky; yet the sun now and then breaks through, appearing like the avenging eye of Jehovah. Fierce lightnings leap from the heavens, enveloping the earth in a sheet of flame. Above the terrific roar of thunder, voices, mysterious and awful, declare the doom of the wicked. The words spoken are not comprehended by all; but they are distinctly understood by the false teachers. Those who a little before were so reckless, so boastful and defiant, so exultant in their cruelty to God's commandment-keeping people, are now overwhelmed with consternation, and shuddering in fear. Their wails are heard above the sound of the elements. Demons acknowledge the divinity of Christ, and tremble before His power, while men are supplicating for mercy, and groveling in abject terror. . . .

"Through a rift in the clouds, there beams a star whose brilliancy is increased fourfold in contrast with the darkness. It speaks hope and joy to the faithful, but severity and wrath to the transgressors of God's law. Those who have sacrificed all for Christ are now secure, hidden as in the secret of the Lord's pavilion. They have been tested, and before the world and the despisers of truth they have evinced their fidelity to Him who died for them. A marvelous change has come over those who have held fast their integrity in the very face of death. They have been suddenly delivered from the dark and terrible tyranny of men transformed to demons. Their faces, so lately pale, anxious, and haggard, are now aglow with wonder, faith, and love. Their voices rise in triumphant song: 'God is our refuge and strength, a very present help in trouble. Therefore will not we fear, though the earth be removed, and though the mountains be carried into the midst of the sea; though the waters thereof roar and be troubled, though the mountains shake with the swelling thereof.'

"While these words of holy trust ascend to God, the clouds sweep back, and the starry heavens are seen, unspeakably glorious in contrast with the black and angry firmament on either side. The glory of the celestial city streams from the gates ajar. Then there appears against the sky a hand holding two tables of stone folded together. Says the prophet, 'The heavens shall declare His righteousness; for God is judge Himself.' That holy law, God's righteousness, that amid thunder and flame was proclaimed from Sinai as the guide of life, is now revealed to men as the rule of judgment. The hand opens the tables, and there are seen the precepts of the decalogue, traced as with a pen of fire. The words are so plain that all can read them. Memory is aroused, the darkness of superstition and heresy is swept from every mind, and God's ten words, brief, comprehensive, and authoritative, are presented to the view of all the inhabitants of the earth.

"It is impossible to describe the horror and despair of those who have trampled upon God's holy requrements. The Lord gave them His law; they might have compared their characters with it, and learned their defects while there was yet opportunity for repentance and reform; but in order to secure the favor of the world, they set aside its precepts and taught others to transgress. They have endeavored to compel God's people to profane His Sabbath. Now they are condemned by that law which they have despised. With awful distinctness they see that they are without excuse. They chose whom they would serve and worship. 'Then shall ye return, and discern between the righteous and the wicked, between him that serveth God and him that serveth him not.'

"The enemies of God's law, from the ministers down to the least among them, have a new conception of truth and duty. Too late they see that the Sabbath of the fourth commandment is the seal of the living God. Too late they see the true nature of their spurious sabbath, and the sandy foundation upon which they have been building. They find that they have been fighting against God. Religious teachers have led souls to perdition while professing to guide them to the gates of Paradise. Not until the day of final accounts will it be known how great is the responsibility of men in holy office, and how terrible are the results of their unfaithfulness. Only in eternity can we rightly estimate the loss of a single soul. Fearful will be the doom of him to whom God shall say, Depart, thou wicked servant.

"The voice of God is heard from Heaven, declaring the day and hour of Jesus' coming, and delivering the everlasting covenant to His people. Like peals of loudest thunder, His words roll through the earth. The Israel of God stand listening, with their eyes fixed upward. Their countenances are lighted up with His glory, and shine as did the face of Moses when he came down from Sinai. The wicked cannot look upon them. And when the blessing is pronounced on those who have honored God by keeping His Sabbath holy, there is a mighty shout of victory.

"Soon there appears in the east a small black cloud, about half the size of a man's hand. It is the cloud which surrounds the Saviour, and which seems in the distance to be shrouded in darkness. The people of

God know this to be the sign of the Son of man. In solemn silence they gaze upon it as it draws nearer the earth, becoming lighter and more glorious, until it is a great white cloud, its base a glory like consuming fire, and above it the rainbow of the covenant. Jesus rides forth as a mighty conqueror. Not now a 'man of sorrows,' to drink the bitter cup of shame and woe, He comes, Victor in Heaven and earth, to judge the living and the dead. 'Faithful and True,' 'in righteousness He doth judge and make war.' And 'the armies in Heaven follow Him.' With anthems of celestial melody the holy angels, a vast, unnumbered throng, attend Him on His way. The firmament seems filled with radiant forms, -- 'ten thousand times ten thousand, and thousands of thousands.' No human pen can portray the scene, nor mortal mind is adequate to conceive its splendor. 'His glory covered the heavens, and the earth was full of His praise. And His brightness was as the light.' As the living cloud comes still nearer, every eye beholds the Prince of life. No crown of thorns now mars that sacred head, but a diadem of glory rests on His holy brow. His countenance outshines the dazzling brightness of the noonday sun. 'And He hath on His vesture and on His thigh a name written, KING OF KINGS, AND LORD OF LORDS.' . . .

"The King of kings descends upon the cloud, wrapped in flaming fire. The heavens are rolled together as a scroll, the earth trembles before Him, and every mountain and island is moved out of its place. 'Our God shall come, and shall not keep silence; a fire shall devour before Him, and it shall be very tempestuous round about Him. He shall call to the heavens from above, and to the earth, that He may judge His people.' . . .

"And the kings of the earth, and the great men, and the rich men, and the chief captains, and the mighty men, and every bondman, and every freeman, hid themselves in the dens and in the rocks, Fall on us, and hide us from the face of Him that sitteth on the throne, and from the wrath of the Lamb; for the great day of His wrath is come; and who shall be able to stand?'" . . .

"Amid the reeling of the earth, the flash of lightning, and the roar of thunder, the voice of the Son of God calls forth the sleeping saints. He looks upon the graves of the righteous, then raising His hands to heaven He cries, 'Awake, awake, awake, ye that sleep in the dust, and arise!' Throughout the length and breadth of the earth, the dead shall hear that voice; and they that hear shall live. And the whole earth shall ring with the tread of the exceeding great army of every nation, kindred, tongue, and people. From the prison-house of death they come, clothed with immortal glory, crying, 'O death, where is thy sting? O grave, where is thy victory?' And the living righteous and the risen saints unite their voices in a long, glad shout of victory.

"All come forth from their graves the same in stature as when they entered the tomb. Adam, who stands smong the risen throng, is of lofty height and majestic form, in stature but little below the Son of God. He presents a marked contrast to the people of later generations; in this one respect is shown the great degeneracy of the race. But all arise with the freshness and vigor of eternal youth. In the beginning, man was created in the likeness of God, not only in character, but in form and feature. Sin defaced and almost obliterated the divine image; but Christ came to restore that which had been lost. He will change our vile bodies, and fashion them like unto His glorious body. The mortal, corruptible form, devoid of comeliness, once polluted with sin, becomes perfect, beautiful, and immortal. All blemishes and deformities are left in the grave. Restored to the tree of life in the long-lost Eden, the redeemed will 'grow up' to the full stature of the race in its primeval glory. The last lingering traces of the curse of sin will be removed, and Christ's faithful ones will appear 'in the beauty of the Lord our God;' in mind and soul and body reflecting the perfect image of their Lord. Oh, wonderful redemption! long talked of, long hoped for, contemplated with eager anticipation, but never fully understood.

"The living righteous are changed 'in a moment, in the twinkling of an eye.' At the voice of God they were glorified; now they are made immortal, and with the risen saints are caught up to meet their Lord in the air. Angels "gather together the elect from the four winds, from one end of heaven to the other." Little children are borne by holy angels to their mothers' arms. Friends long separated by death are united, nevermore to part, and with songs of gladness ascend together to the city of God. . . .

"Before entering the city of God, the Saviour bestows upon His followers the emblems of victory, and invests them with the insignia of their royal state. The glittering ranks are drawn up, in the form of a hollow square, about their King, whose form rises in majesty high above saint and angel, whose countenance beams upon them full of benignant love. Throughout the unnumbered host of the redeemed; every glance is fixed upon Him, every eye beholds His glory whose 'visage was so marred more than any man, and His form more than the sons of men.' Upon the heads of the overcomers, Jesus with His own right hand places the crown of glory. For each there is a crown, bearing His own 'new name,' and the inscription, 'Holiness to the Lord.' In every hand are placed the victor's palm and the shining harp. Then, as the commanding angels strike the note, every hand sweeps the harp strings with skillful touch, awaking sweet music in rich, melodious strains. Rapture unutterable thrills every heart, and each voice is raised in grateful praise: 'Unto Him that loved us, and washed us from our sins in His own blood, and hath made us kings and priests unto God and His Father; to Him be glory and dominion forever and ever.'

"Before the ransomed throng is the holy city. Jesus opens wide the pearly gates, and the nations that have kept the truth enter in. There they behold the Paradise of God, the home of Adam in his innocency. Then that voice, richer than any music that ever fell on mortal ear, is heard, saying, 'Your conflict is ended.' 'Come, ye blessed of My Father, inherit the kingdom prepared for you from the foundation of the world.'

"Now is fulfilled the Saviour's prayer for His disciples, 'I will that they also whom Thou has given Me be with Me where I am.' 'Faultless before the presence of His glory with exceeding joy,' Christ presents to the Father the purchase of His blood, declaring, 'Here am I, and the children whom Thou has given Me.' 'Those that Thou gavest Me I have kept.' Oh, the wonders of redeeming love! the rapture of that hour when the infinite Father, looking upon the ransomed, shall behold His image, sin's discord banished, its blight removed, and the human once more in harmony with the divine!"

"With unutterable love, Jesus welcomes His faithful ones to the 'joy of their Lord.' The Saviour's joy is in seeing, in the kingdom of glory, the souls that have been saved by His agony and humiliation. And the redeemed will be sharers in this joy, as they behold, among the blessed, those who have been won to Christ through their prayers, their labors, and loving sacrifice. As they gather about the great white throne, gladness unspeakable will fill their hearts, when they behold those whom they have won for Christ, and see that one has gained others, and these still others, all brought into the haven of rest, there to lay their crowns at Jesus' feet, and praise Him through the endless cycles of eternity."

~ True of False ~

[] T [] F When the protection of human laws shall be withdrawn from those who honor the law of God, there will be a simultaneous movement for their destruction.

[] T [] F It is at midnight that God manifests His power for the deliverance of His people.

[] T [] F All who have died in the faith of the third's angel's message come forth from the tomb glorified, to hear God's covenant of peace with those who have kept His law.

[] T [] F Those who mocked and derided Christ's dying agonies will be resurrected at His coming to behold Him in His glory.

[] T [] F The holy law of God will be presented to the view of all the inhabitants of the earth.

[] T [] F After viewing the law of God, those who never accepted the law will realize, when Christ comes their error and repent.

[] T [] F Only in eternity can we rightly estimate the loss of a single soul.

[] T [] F God will reveal the day and hour of Jesus' coming.

[] T [] F There is a quiet calmness among the redeemed as the blessing is pronounced on them by God for keeping His Sabbath holy.

[] T [] F The small black cloud, about the size of a man's hand, that will appear will become lighter and more glorious as it gets closer to the earth.

[] T [] F Every eye shall see Jesus when He comes.

[] T [] F   Some of the righteous will be so frighten they when Jesus returns they will try to hide in the dens and the rocks.

[] T [] F   The sound of the trumpet of Jesus shall awaken the dead saints.

[] T [] F   All come forth from their graves the same in stature as when they entered the tomb.

[] T [] F   Jesus will change our vile bodies and fashion them like unto His glorious body.

[] T [] F   Christ's faithful ones will appear in the beauty of the Lord our God in mind and soul as well as body.

[] T [] F   The change of the redeemed will only take seven days.

[] T [] F   The emblems of victory Jesus will bestow on His followers are the crowns of glory.

[] T [] F   All crowns of glory will contain the new names of the redeemed.

[] T [] F   The angels will teach the redeemed to play their harp.

[] T [] F   Jesus' prayer will be fulfilled "I will that they also whom Thou has given Me be with Me where I am."

CHAPTER 13

PREPARATION FOR THE CRISIS

"Thy Word have I hid in mine heart, that I might not sin against Thee."

Psalm 119:11

Chapter 13

Preparation for the Crisis

Write out John 5:39

_____

_____

_____

_____

_____

Complete the following statement quoted on page 163:

"My brethren, do you _____ that your own _____, as well as the _____ of other _____, depends upon the _____ you _____ make for the _____ before us? Have you that intensity of _____, that _____ and devotion, which will _____ you to _____ when opposition shall be brought against you? If _____ has ever spoken by me, the time will come when _____ will be brought before _____, and every position of _____ which you hold will be severely _____. The time that so many are now _____ to go to _____ should be _____ to the charge that _____ has given us of _____ for the approaching _____."

-- Testimonies to the Church, volume 5, page 716-717

Chapter 13 - Preparation for the Crisis

Personal: How can I prepare the children under my influence for the great crisis?

_____
_____
_____
_____

> Please answer the following questions as they relate to the six "Factors in the Preparation" as outlined in the text.

1. Study of the Bible and the spirit of prophecy

Write out II Timothy 2:15

_____
_____
_____
_____

Personal: In what areas of my faith do I need a clearer understanding? How will I <u>now</u> go about obtaining a clearer understanding in these areas?

_____
_____
_____
_____

Do you know what you believe in the following three areas of your faith and can you give evidence of your beliefs from Scripture?

Belief	Scripture Support	Scripture Support	Scripture Support
State of the Dead			
Three Angels' Message			
Investigative Judgment			
Sanctification			
Justification			

Read Ephesians 6:13-17 and define each item in the armor of God:

Girdle _____
_____
_____

Breast-plate _____
_____
_____

Shoes _____
_____
_____

Shield _____
_____
_____

Helmet _____
_____
_____

Sword _____
_____
_____

Study Work Book for "Preparation for the Final Crisis"

2. Communion with God; fervent prayer

Write out II Thessalonians 5:17

_____

_____

_____

_____

Complete the following statement quoted on page 166:

"As the _____ ones continued their earnest _____, at times a ray of _____ from _____ came to them, to _____ their hearts and light up their _____. Some, I saw, did not _____ in this work of _____ and pleading. They seemed _____ and _____. They were not _____ the darkness around them, and it _____ them in like a _____ cloud. The _____ of God _____ these and went to the _____ of the earnest, _____ ones. I saw _____ of God hasten to the _____ of all who were _____ with all their power to resist the _____ angels and trying to _____ themselves by calling upon God with _____. But His angels _____ those who made no _____ to help _____ and I lost _____ of them." -- Early Writings, page 270.

Personal: How do I need to adjust my life to incorporate more time for prayer?

_____

_____

_____

_____

3. Cleansing from sin and victory over weaknesses

Write out I John 1:9

_____

_____

_____

_____

Complete the following statement quoted on page 167:

"Satan _____ many to _____ that God will overlook their unfaithfulness in the _____ affairs of life; but the _____ shows in His dealings with Jacob that He will in _____ wise _____ or tolerate _____. All who endeavor to _____ or conceal their _____, and _____ them to remain upon the _____ of heaven, _____ and _____, will be _____ by Satan." -- Great Controversy, page 620

Personal: What do I need to do to remedy the defects in my character?

_____

_____

_____

_____

_____

_____

4. A complete surrender to God

Write II Peter 2:9

_____

_____

_____

_____

Complete the following statement quoted on page 168:

"Consecrate yourself to God in the _____; make this your very _____ work. Let your _____ be, 'Take me, O Lord, as _____ Thine. I lay _____ my _____ at Thy _____. Use me _____ in Thy _____. Abide with _____, and let _____ my work be wrought in _____.' This is a _____ matter. Each morning _____ yourself to God for _____ day. Surrender _____ your plans to _____, to be _____ out or _____ up as _____ providence shall indicate. Thus _____ by _____ you may be _____ your _____ into the _____ of God, and thus your _____ will be _____ more and more _____ the life of _____." -- Steps to Christ, page 70

"If all had a sense of the conflict which each soul must wage with satanic agencies that are seeking to ensnare, entice, and deceive, there would be much more diligent labor for those who are young in the faith." -- 6T, 92-93

Personal: What can **I** do to encourage those who are young in the faith?

_____

_____

_____

Study Work Book for "Preparation for the Final Crisis"

5. A diligent work for Christ

Write Matthew 5:16

_____

_____

_____

_____

Complete the following statement quoted on page 169:

"We have _____ time to lose. The _____ is near. The _____ from place to place to _____ the truth will _____ be hedged with _____ on the right _____ and on the left. Everything will be placed to _____ the way of the Lord's _____, so that they will not be able to do that which it is _____ for them to do _____. We must look our work _____ in the face and _____ as fast as possible in _____ warfare." -- Testimonies to the Church, volume 6, page 22

"Christ has committed to your trust talents of means and of influence, and He has said to you: Improve these till I come." -- 4T 51

Personal: How can I improve and use the talents God has given me to further His work?

_____

_____

_____

_____

6. Activity on behalf of religious liberty

Write out James 3:17-18

_____
_____
_____
_____
_____
_____

<u>Complete the following statement quoted on page 170</u>:

"We as a _____ have not accomplished the _____ which God has _____ to us. We are not _____ for the _____ to which the _____ of the _____ law will bring us. It is our _____, as we see the _____ of approaching _____, to arouse to _____. Let none _____ in calm _____. . . . Let there be most earnest _____, and then let us work in _____ with our _____." -- Testimonies to the Church, pages 713-714

Write out Revelation 22:12

_____
_____
_____

APPENDIX

End Time Books and Resources

Title	Author
The New World Order	Russell Burrill
Preparation for the Final Crisis	Fernando Chaij
Day of the Dragon	Clifford Goldstein
The Antichrist and the New World Order	Marvin Moore
The Crisis of the End Time	Marvin Moore
Countdown to the Showdown	Dwight K. Nelson
Countdown to the Showdown Study Guide	Dwight K. Nelson
The Crisis Ahead	Robert W. Olson
Study Outlines for Preparation for the Final Crisis	C. J. Ritchie
The Great Controversy	Ellen G. White
Last Day Events	Ellen G. White
Maranatha	Ellen G. White
Promises for the Last Days	Ellen G. White

To order these books contact your local Adventist Book Center.

MARANATHA!

*Even so,
Come Lord Jesus!*